WHEN LIFE ~~THROWS~~ YOU A ~~CURVE~~ LEAN INTO IT

THIS MILEAGE LOG BOOK
BELONGS TO:

_____

_____

_____

MAKE:		MODEL:		YEAR:

DATE	ODOMETER		TOTAL	DESTINATION
	START	END		

TOTAL MILEAGE:

MAKE:		MODEL:		YEAR:

DATE	ODOMETER 🕭		TOTAL	DESTINATION
	START	END		

TOTAL MILEAGE:

MAKE:		MODEL:		YEAR:
DATE	**ODOMETER** 🔘		**TOTAL**	**DESTINATION**
	START	**END**		

TOTAL MILEAGE:

MAKE:		MODEL:		YEAR:
DATE	ODOMETER 🕑		TOTAL	DESTINATION
	START	END		

TOTAL MILEAGE:

MAKE:		MODEL:		YEAR:

DATE	ODOMETER 🕭		TOTAL	DESTINATION
	START	END		

TOTAL MILEAGE:

MAKE:	MODEL:			YEAR:
DATE	ODOMETER 🕸		TOTAL	DESTINATION
	START	END		
TOTAL MILEAGE:				

MAKE:		MODEL:		YEAR:

| DATE | ODOMETER | | TOTAL | DESTINATION |
	START	END		

TOTAL MILEAGE:

MAKE:		MODEL:		YEAR:
DATE	**ODOMETER** 🕐		**TOTAL**	**DESTINATION**
	START	**END**		

TOTAL MILEAGE:

MAKE:		MODEL:		YEAR:

DATE	ODOMETER		TOTAL	DESTINATION
	START	END		

TOTAL MILEAGE:

MAKE:		MODEL:		YEAR:

DATE	ODOMETER		TOTAL	DESTINATION
	START	END		

TOTAL MILEAGE:

MAKE:		MODEL:		YEAR:
DATE	**ODOMETER** 🕭		**TOTAL**	**DESTINATION**
	START	**END**		
TOTAL MILEAGE:				

MAKE:		MODEL:		YEAR:

DATE	ODOMETER 🕥		TOTAL	DESTINATION
	START	END		

TOTAL MILEAGE:

MAKE:	MODEL:			YEAR:
DATE	ODOMETER		TOTAL	DESTINATION
	START	END		
TOTAL MILEAGE:				

MAKE:		MODEL:		YEAR:

| DATE | ODOMETER 🕬 | | TOTAL | DESTINATION |
	START	END		

TOTAL MILEAGE:

MAKE:		MODEL:		YEAR:
DATE	**ODOMETER** 🕐		**TOTAL**	**DESTINATION**
	START	**END**		
TOTAL MILEAGE:				

MAKE:		MODEL:		YEAR:

DATE	ODOMETER 🔘		TOTAL	DESTINATION
	START	END		

TOTAL MILEAGE:

MAKE:		MODEL:		YEAR:
DATE	**ODOMETER** 🔘		**TOTAL**	**DESTINATION**
	START	**END**		

TOTAL MILEAGE:

MAKE:		MODEL:		YEAR:
DATE	**ODOMETER** 🔊		**TOTAL**	**DESTINATION**
	START	**END**		

TOTAL MILEAGE:

MAKE:		MODEL:		YEAR:

DATE	ODOMETER 🕮		TOTAL	DESTINATION
	START	END		

TOTAL MILEAGE:

MAKE:			MODEL:		YEAR:

DATE	ODOMETER		TOTAL	DESTINATION
	START	END		

TOTAL MILEAGE:

MAKE:		MODEL:		YEAR:
DATE	ODOMETER		TOTAL	DESTINATION
	START	END		

TOTAL MILEAGE:

MAKE: **MODEL:**   **YEAR:**

DATE	ODOMETER		TOTAL	DESTINATION
	START	END		

TOTAL MILEAGE:

MAKE:		MODEL:		YEAR:
DATE	ODOMETER		TOTAL	DESTINATION
	START	END		
TOTAL MILEAGE:				

MAKE:		MODEL:		YEAR:

DATE	ODOMETER 🕿		TOTAL	DESTINATION
	START	END		

TOTAL MILEAGE:

MAKE:		MODEL:		YEAR:
DATE	ODOMETER		TOTAL	DESTINATION
	START	END		
TOTAL MILEAGE:				

MAKE:		MODEL:		YEAR:
DATE	ODOMETER 🕐		TOTAL	DESTINATION
	START	END		

TOTAL MILEAGE:

MAKE:		MODEL:		YEAR:
DATE	ODOMETER 🕐		TOTAL	DESTINATION
	START	END		
TOTAL MILEAGE:				

MAKE:		MODEL:		YEAR:

DATE	ODOMETER		TOTAL	DESTINATION
	START	END		

TOTAL MILEAGE:

MAKE:		MODEL:		YEAR:
DATE	ODOMETER		TOTAL	DESTINATION
	START	END		
TOTAL MILEAGE:				

MAKE:		MODEL:		YEAR:
DATE	ODOMETER		TOTAL	DESTINATION
	START	END		

TOTAL MILEAGE:

MAKE:		MODEL:		YEAR:
DATE	**ODOMETER** 🝢		**TOTAL**	**DESTINATION**
	START	**END**		

TOTAL MILEAGE:

MAKE:		MODEL:		YEAR:
DATE	**ODOMETER** 🔘		**TOTAL**	**DESTINATION**
	START	**END**		
TOTAL MILEAGE:				

MAKE:		MODEL:		YEAR:
DATE	**ODOMETER** 🕸		**TOTAL**	**DESTINATION**
	START	**END**		
TOTAL MILEAGE:				

MAKE:		MODEL:		YEAR:
DATE	**ODOMETER** 🝵		**TOTAL**	**DESTINATION**
	START	**END**		

TOTAL MILEAGE:

MAKE:		MODEL:		YEAR:
DATE	**ODOMETER**		**TOTAL**	**DESTINATION**
	START	**END**		
TOTAL MILEAGE:				

MAKE:		MODEL:		YEAR:
DATE	**ODOMETER** 🔘		**TOTAL**	**DESTINATION**
	START	**END**		

TOTAL MILEAGE:

MAKE:		MODEL:		YEAR:
DATE	ODOMETER		TOTAL	DESTINATION
	START	END		
TOTAL MILEAGE:				

MAKE:		MODEL:		YEAR:

DATE	ODOMETER 🕭		TOTAL	DESTINATION
	START	END		

TOTAL MILEAGE:

MAKE:		MODEL:		YEAR:

DATE	ODOMETER		TOTAL	DESTINATION
	START	END		

TOTAL MILEAGE:

| DATE | ODOMETER | | TOTAL | DESTINATION |
	START	END		

MAKE: **MODEL:**   **YEAR:**

TOTAL MILEAGE:

MAKE:		MODEL:		YEAR:
DATE	**ODOMETER**		**TOTAL**	**DESTINATION**
	START	**END**		
TOTAL MILEAGE:				

MAKE:		MODEL:		YEAR:
DATE	**ODOMETER** 🕐		**TOTAL**	**DESTINATION**
	START	**END**		
TOTAL MILEAGE:				

MAKE:		MODEL:		YEAR:
DATE	ODOMETER		TOTAL	DESTINATION
	START	END		
TOTAL MILEAGE:				

MAKE:		MODEL:		YEAR:
DATE	ODOMETER 🌀		TOTAL	DESTINATION
	START	END		
TOTAL MILEAGE:				

MAKE:		MODEL:		YEAR:
DATE	**ODOMETER**		**TOTAL**	**DESTINATION**
	START	**END**		
TOTAL MILEAGE:				

MAKE:		MODEL:		YEAR:

DATE	ODOMETER		TOTAL	DESTINATION
	START	END		

TOTAL MILEAGE:

MAKE:		MODEL:		YEAR:
DATE	ODOMETER 🕭		TOTAL	DESTINATION
	START	END		
TOTAL MILEAGE:				

MAKE:		MODEL:		YEAR:
DATE	ODOMETER		TOTAL	DESTINATION
	START	END		
TOTAL MILEAGE:				

MAKE:		MODEL:		YEAR:
DATE	**ODOMETER** 🔘		**TOTAL**	**DESTINATION**
	START	**END**		
TOTAL MILEAGE:				

MAKE:		MODEL:		YEAR:
DATE	ODOMETER 🕭		TOTAL	DESTINATION
	START	END		
TOTAL MILEAGE:				

MAKE:		MODEL:		YEAR:
DATE	ODOMETER 🕑		TOTAL	DESTINATION
	START	END		

TOTAL MILEAGE:

MAKE:		MODEL:		YEAR:

DATE	ODOMETER		TOTAL	DESTINATION
	START	END		

TOTAL MILEAGE:

MAKE:		MODEL:		YEAR:
DATE	**ODOMETER**		**TOTAL**	**DESTINATION**
	START	**END**		

TOTAL MILEAGE:

MAKE:		MODEL:		YEAR:
DATE	**ODOMETER** 🕰		**TOTAL**	**DESTINATION**
	START	**END**		
TOTAL MILEAGE:				

MAKE: **MODEL:**   **YEAR:**

DATE	ODOMETER		TOTAL	DESTINATION
	START	END		

TOTAL MILEAGE:

MAKE:		MODEL:		YEAR:

DATE	ODOMETER 🔲		TOTAL	DESTINATION
	START	END		

TOTAL MILEAGE:

MAKE:		MODEL:		YEAR:
DATE	**ODOMETER** 🔲		**TOTAL**	**DESTINATION**
	START	**END**		
TOTAL MILEAGE:				

MAKE:		MODEL:		YEAR:
DATE	ODOMETER 🔍		TOTAL	DESTINATION
	START	END		
TOTAL MILEAGE:				

MAKE:		MODEL:		YEAR:
DATE	ODOMETER 🕰		TOTAL	DESTINATION
	START	END		
TOTAL MILEAGE:				

MAKE:		MODEL:		YEAR:
DATE	ODOMETER		TOTAL	DESTINATION
	START	END		
TOTAL MILEAGE:				

MAKE:		MODEL:		YEAR:
DATE	ODOMETER		TOTAL	DESTINATION
	START	END		
TOTAL MILEAGE:				

MAKE:		MODEL:		YEAR:
DATE	**ODOMETER**		**TOTAL**	**DESTINATION**
	START	**END**		

TOTAL MILEAGE:

MAKE:		MODEL:		YEAR:
DATE	ODOMETER 🔉		TOTAL	DESTINATION
	START	END		
TOTAL MILEAGE:				

MAKE:		MODEL:		YEAR:
DATE	ODOMETER 🕓		TOTAL	DESTINATION
	START	END		
TOTAL MILEAGE:				

MAKE:			MODEL:		YEAR:
DATE	**ODOMETER** 🔘		**TOTAL**	**DESTINATION**	
	START	**END**			

TOTAL MILEAGE:

MAKE:		MODEL:		YEAR:

DATE	ODOMETER 🔾		TOTAL	DESTINATION
	START	END		

TOTAL MILEAGE:

MAKE:		MODEL:		YEAR:
DATE	ODOMETER		TOTAL	DESTINATION
	START	END		

TOTAL MILEAGE:

MAKE:			MODEL:	YEAR:
DATE	**ODOMETER**		**TOTAL**	**DESTINATION**
	START	**END**		

TOTAL MILEAGE:

MAKE:		MODEL:		YEAR:
DATE	**ODOMETER** 🕑		**TOTAL**	**DESTINATION**
	START	**END**		
TOTAL MILEAGE:				

MAKE: **MODEL:**   **YEAR:**

DATE	ODOMETER		TOTAL	DESTINATION
	START	END		

TOTAL MILEAGE:

MAKE:		MODEL:		YEAR:

DATE	ODOMETER 🕥		TOTAL	DESTINATION
	START	END		

TOTAL MILEAGE:

MAKE:		MODEL:		YEAR:

DATE	ODOMETER 🕑		TOTAL	DESTINATION
	START	END		

TOTAL MILEAGE:

MAKE:		MODEL:		YEAR:

DATE	ODOMETER		TOTAL	DESTINATION
	START	END		

TOTAL MILEAGE:

MAKE:		MODEL:		YEAR:
DATE	**ODOMETER** 🏁		**TOTAL**	**DESTINATION**
	START	**END**		
TOTAL MILEAGE:				

MAKE:		MODEL:		YEAR:
DATE	**ODOMETER** 🔲		**TOTAL**	**DESTINATION**
	START	**END**		

TOTAL MILEAGE:

MAKE:		MODEL:		YEAR:
DATE	ODOMETER		TOTAL	DESTINATION
	START	END		
TOTAL MILEAGE:				

MAKE:		MODEL:		YEAR:

DATE	ODOMETER 🕑		TOTAL	DESTINATION
	START	END		

TOTAL MILEAGE:

MAKE: **MODEL:** **YEAR:**

| DATE | ODOMETER 🔿 | | TOTAL | DESTINATION |
	START	END		

TOTAL MILEAGE:

MAKE:		MODEL:		YEAR:
DATE	**ODOMETER**		**TOTAL**	**DESTINATION**
	START	**END**		
TOTAL MILEAGE:				

DATE	ODOMETER		TOTAL	DESTINATION
	START	END		

MAKE:　　　　**MODEL:**　　　　**YEAR:**

ODOMETER

TOTAL MILEAGE:

MAKE:		MODEL:		YEAR:
DATE	**ODOMETER**		**TOTAL**	**DESTINATION**
	START	**END**		
TOTAL MILEAGE:				

MAKE:		MODEL:		YEAR:
DATE	ODOMETER 🕭		TOTAL	DESTINATION
	START	END		
TOTAL MILEAGE:				

MAKE:		MODEL:		YEAR:
DATE	ODOMETER		TOTAL	DESTINATION
	START	END		
TOTAL MILEAGE:				

MAKE:		MODEL:		YEAR:

DATE	ODOMETER 🌀		TOTAL	DESTINATION
	START	END		

TOTAL MILEAGE:

MAKE:			MODEL:		YEAR:
DATE	**ODOMETER**		**TOTAL**	**DESTINATION**	
	START	**END**			
TOTAL MILEAGE:					

MAKE:		MODEL:		YEAR:
DATE	ODOMETER		TOTAL	DESTINATION
	START	END		
TOTAL MILEAGE:				

MAKE:		MODEL:		YEAR:
DATE	**ODOMETER** 🕐		**TOTAL**	**DESTINATION**
	START	**END**		
TOTAL MILEAGE:				

MAKE:			MODEL:		YEAR:

DATE	ODOMETER		TOTAL	DESTINATION
	START	END		

TOTAL MILEAGE:

MAKE: **MODEL:**   **YEAR:**

DATE	ODOMETER		TOTAL	DESTINATION
	START	END		

TOTAL MILEAGE:

MAKE:	MODEL:			YEAR:
DATE	ODOMETER 🌀		TOTAL	DESTINATION
	START	END		
TOTAL MILEAGE:				

MAKE:		MODEL:		YEAR:
DATE	ODOMETER 🕑		TOTAL	DESTINATION
	START	END		
TOTAL MILEAGE:				

DATE	ODOMETER		TOTAL	DESTINATION
	START	END		
MAKE:		MODEL:		YEAR:

MAKE: **MODEL:**   **YEAR:**

DATE	ODOMETER		TOTAL	DESTINATION
	START	END		

TOTAL MILEAGE:

| DATE | ODOMETER | | TOTAL | DESTINATION |
	START	END		
MAKE:			MODEL:	YEAR:

| DATE | ODOMETER | | TOTAL | DESTINATION |
	START	END		

TOTAL MILEAGE:

MAKE:	MODEL:			YEAR:
DATE	ODOMETER 🕐		TOTAL	DESTINATION
	START	END		
TOTAL MILEAGE:				

MAKE:		MODEL:		YEAR:
DATE	ODOMETER		TOTAL	DESTINATION
	START	END		
TOTAL MILEAGE:				

MAKE:		MODEL:		YEAR:
DATE	ODOMETER 🔘		TOTAL	DESTINATION
	START	END		
TOTAL MILEAGE:				

MAKE:		MODEL:		YEAR:
DATE	**ODOMETER** 🔢		**TOTAL**	**DESTINATION**
	START	**END**		
TOTAL MILEAGE:				

	ODOMETER			
MAKE:		MODEL:		YEAR:

DATE	ODOMETER 🜨		TOTAL	DESTINATION
	START	END		

TOTAL MILEAGE:

MAKE:		MODEL:		YEAR:
DATE	**ODOMETER** 🌀		**TOTAL**	**DESTINATION**
	START	**END**		
TOTAL MILEAGE:				

MAKE:		MODEL:		YEAR:

DATE	ODOMETER		TOTAL	DESTINATION
	START	END		

TOTAL MILEAGE:

Made in the USA
Monee, IL
24 January 2023